COLIN KAEPERNICK

BY PAUL HOBLIN

Printed in the United States of America,
North Mankato, Minnesota
052013
012014

 THIS BOOK CONTAINS AT LEAST 10% RECYCLED MATERIALS.

Editor: Chrös McDougall
Series Designer: Craig Hinton

Photo Credits: Greg Trott/AP Images, cover, 1, 8; Kevin Terrell/AP Images, 4; Ben Liebenberg/AP Images, 7; Elaine Thompson/AP Images, 10; Marcio Jose Sanchez/AP Images, 13, 21; Matt York/AP Images, 14; Matt Cilley/AP Images, 17; Idaho Statesman - Joe Jaszewski/AP Images, 18; Damian Strohmeyer/AP Images, 22; Ric Tapia/AP Images, 25; Tom Hauck/AP Images, 26; Jed Jacobsohn/AP Images, 29

Library of Congress Control Number: 2013934742

Cataloging-in-Publication Data

Hoblin, Paul.
 Colin Kaepernick: NFL phenom / Paul Hoblin.
   p. cm. -- (Playmakers)
ISBN 978-1-61783-701-2
1. Kaepernick, Colin, 1987- --Juvenile literature. 2. Football players--United States--Biography--Juvenile literature. 3. Quarterbacks (Football)--United States--Biography--Juvenile literature. I. Title.
796.332092--dc23
 [B]   2013934742

TABLE OF CONTENTS

Colin Kaepernick

CHAPTER 1

THIS KID'S GOT AN ARM!

National Football League (NFL) teams usually do not like to rely on young quarterbacks in big games. But that is exactly what the San Francisco 49ers were doing on January 12, 2013. Colin Kaepernick was starting a playoff game against the Green Bay Packers.

The Packers were one of the best teams in the NFL. The pressure was on Colin to lead his team against a great opponent on a huge stage.

Colin Kaepernick sets up to pass against the Green Bay Packers during a January 2013 playoff game.

Packers star quarterback Aaron Rodgers played well, leading his team to 31 points. But Colin played even better. He threw two touchdowns. And he did even more damage with his legs. By the end of the game he had rushed for two touchdowns and 181 yards. That was the most rushing yards by any quarterback in NFL playoff history. Most importantly, Colin's heroics helped his team win the game, 45–31.

Colin was born on November 3, 1987, in Milwaukee, Wisconsin. His parents told him early in life that he was adopted. And they told him that this was a good thing. They said they were lucky to call him their son.

This explanation was good enough for Colin. When he drew pictures of his family at school, his classmates would ask him why he was a different color than the rest of the family.

When Colin was 10 years old, he got a pet tortoise named Sammy. It was still alive when Colin played in Super Bowl XLVII in 2013. Sammy now weighs more than 100 pounds.

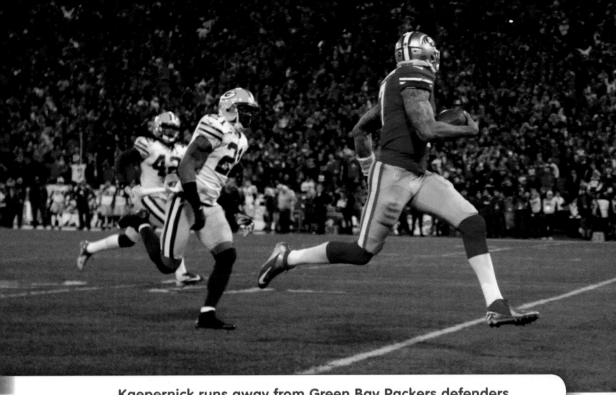

Kaepernick runs away from Green Bay Packers defenders during the playoffs after the 2012 season.

That is because Colin's parents are white and he is biracial. One of his birth parents was African American and the other was white. In response to his classmates, Colin would just shrug and laugh. He did not care that he looked a little different from his family. He just cared that they were his family.

When Colin was four, his family moved from Fond du Lac, Wisconsin, to Turlock, California. A few years after that, Colin started playing football.

Growing up, Kaepernick dreamed of playing for the San Francisco 49ers.

He started out as the team's punter even though he did not have a great leg. What he did have was a great arm. He would win Punt, Pass, and Kick competitions because he could throw the ball so much farther than anyone else his age. The people measuring the contestants' throws would stand far away. That way, they could see exactly where the balls landed. But Colin would still throw it over their heads.

By the time he was nine, Colin was his team's starting quarterback. The first pass he threw was a touchdown. Children and their parents were not used to seeing another child throw that far.

It was around this time that Colin was given a school assignment. He was asked to write a letter about what he wanted to be when he grew up. Colin wrote that he wanted to play for either the San Francisco 49ers or the Green Bay Packers, even if they were not very good.

Of course, Colin ended up getting his wish. He is now the star quarterback for the 49ers. And it turned out he did not need to worry about the team not being very good. The 49ers are one of the best teams in football—and Colin is one of the reasons they're so good.

In Colin's letter about what he wanted to be when he grew up, he also wrote that he wanted to be more than 6-feet tall. He's now 6-foot-6.

Colin Kaepernick

CHAPTER 2

A YOUNG ATHLETE

Colin attended John H. Pitman High School in Turlock, California. He was a great student and got straight As. One reason for his good grades was his determination. He wanted to be the best at everything.

Colin played basketball growing up. Every day he would challenge one of his teammates to a race. And every day his teammate would win. But that did not stop Colin from challenging him again the next day.

Fans at Super Bowl XLVII saw a tall likeness of Kaepernick on a building in New Orleans.

Even if he was not quite as fast as his teammate, Colin was a really good all-around athlete. He was a star in football, basketball, and baseball. Many considered baseball to be his best sport. Colin was a pitcher who could throw 94 miles per hour. Several big colleges wanted him on their baseball teams. So did the Chicago Cubs. They drafted him in 2009.

But Colin did not want to pitch—not in college or in the pros. He wanted to play football. The only problem was that no one seemed interested in him as a quarterback.

During Colin's senior year, his football coach and his brother put together a highlight video. It included many of Colin's best plays on the football field. They sent it to more than 100 colleges. Not a single one of them responded.

Colin still had not been offered a football scholarship by the end of his senior season. It looked as though his dream of

In high school, Colin was named the Most Valuable Player of the Central California Conference in football. He passed for 1,954 yards and 25 touchdowns.

Kaepernick celebrates with fans after beating the Chicago Bears in a 2012 game.

playing quarterback in college might be over. Then a football coach from the University of Nevada attended a Pitman High School basketball game.

Colin was really sick that day. He had a 102-degree fever. But he played great anyway. The Nevada coach was impressed. Not only was Kaepernick an outstanding athlete, he also was really tough. The Nevada coach had never seen Colin play football. But he decided he wanted Colin to play quarterback for his team.

14 Colin Kaepernick

CHAPTER 3

SIDELINES TO STARDOM

Kaepernick had a great arm, but he threw the football sidearmed. It looked strange. And his coach at Nevada, Chris Ault, thought about moving Kaepernick to another position.

After all, Kaepernick did not only have a great arm. He also was surprisingly fast. Back in high school, his coaches did not want him to run too much because they were afraid he was going to get hurt.

Kaepernick slips past a University of New Mexico tackler during a 2007 game.

At the time, Kaepernick was really skinny. He was slightly more than 6-feet tall but only weighed around 170 pounds. It was not until he got to college that he started to put on muscle.

But Kaepernick did not want to play another position. He wanted to play quarterback. Ault agreed to help him with his throwing motion, but at first he did not let Kaepernick start at quarterback. Kaepernick was redshirted his first year. That meant he was allowed to practice with the team but could not play in games. However, he could still play in games for four seasons after that.

Kaepernick was still on the sidelines at the beginning of the next season, in 2007. During the fifth game of the season, the Nevada starting quarterback went down with an injury against Fresno State. For the first time, Kaepernick was asked to run Nevada's offense. Even though Fresno State won the game, Kaepernick played really well. He threw for 384 yards and four touchdowns. From then on, Kaepernick was Nevada's starting quarterback.

The next week, Nevada played its rival, Boise State University. The game went back and forth. Both teams made a

Kaepernick stretches toward the end zone while being tackled by a Boise State defender in 2007.

lot of big plays. Boise State's kicker made a field goal to send the game to overtime. And as it turned out, one overtime was not enough. Neither were two overtimes—or three.

Finally, in the fourth overtime, Kaepernick was sacked while attempting a two-point conversion. The final score was 67–65. Once again, Kaepernick's team had lost. But by now it was clear that Kaepernick was a star player. In the game, he had thrown

Kaepernick spins away from a Boise State defensive end during a 2010 game in Reno, Nevada.

for 243 yards and rushed for 177 more. He also had thrown and rushed for a combined five touchdowns.

As good as Kaepernick was, he stayed humble. During the summer he worked at a sporting goods store. One day, a customer came in and said she wanted to buy a Nevada Wolf Pack jersey for her son. She asked him if he knew the starting quarterback's number. That is when Kaepernick realized that she did not know who she was talking to. That was okay with him. He sold her the jersey but did not tell her who he was.

By his senior year, Kaepernick had accomplished a lot. For two straight seasons, he had passed for more than 2,000 yards and rushed for more than 1,000. In 2008, he had been named his conference's Player of the Year. But there was one thing Kaepernick still hadn't done: win a game against Boise State.

The 2010 season would be his last chance to beat his rival, and it would not be easy. Boise State entered the game ranked third in the nation. The Broncos had won 24 games in a row. At one point in the first half, they were ahead of Nevada 17–0.

The second half was a different story, though. Nevada's defense started to play better. So did its offense. With five minutes to go in the game, the score was tied 24–24. Boise

Kaepernick was not the only Wolf Pack player who was gaining a lot of yards. His teammate, Vai Taua, also rushed for more than 1,000 yards in three straight seasons. Together, they set a college record for career rushing yards by teammates.

State scored a long touchdown, and it seemed as though the game was all but over. But Kaepernick led his offense down the field and threw a seven-yard touchdown pass, tying the game 31–31.

With only a few seconds left on the clock, Boise State had a chance to win the game with a field goal. But the kicker missed. Once again, the two teams were going to overtime. Boise State's kicker missed another field goal in overtime. Then it was the Wolf Pack's kicker who had a chance to win the game. He made the 34-yard field goal and tore off his helmet to celebrate. Kaepernick and his team had finally beaten Boise State.

Nevada finished the season as co-champions of its conference. The Wolf Pack then went to the Kraft Fight Hunger Bowl. Once again, Kaepernick led his team to victory.

Kaepernick finished eighth in the Heisman Trophy voting his senior year. The Heisman Trophy is given out to the best college football player each season.

Kaepernick runs past a Boston College defensive back during the Kraft Fight Hunger Bowl after the 2010 season.

His college football days were over, but Kaepernick's career had just begun. It was time to start thinking about the NFL. Kaepernick was selected in the second round of the 2011 NFL Draft. He went to none other than his favorite team: the San Francisco 49ers.

Colin Kaepernick

CHAPTER 4

SUPER BACKUP TO SUPER BOWL

Kaepernick did the same thing when he arrived in the NFL that he had done when he arrived at Nevada: he rode the bench. Kaepernick spent most of his first season on the sidelines. After all, the San Francisco 49ers were one of the best teams in the league, and Kaepernick was only a rookie.

Besides, starting quarterback Alex Smith was having a great season. In 2011, Smith helped the 49ers

Kaepernick looks to make a play against the New England Patriots during the 2012 season.

go 13–3 in the regular season. And in the playoffs, he brought them all the way to the conference championship game.

Smith played even better in 2012, so Kaepernick was still the backup. Then, in a Week 10 game against the St. Louis Rams, Smith suffered a concussion.

Just as he had in college, Kaepernick stepped in to replace the injured quarterback. He did not play his best football, but he played well enough not to lose. The game ended in a tie. Still, Kaepernick completed 11 of his 17 passes. And just as importantly, he rushed for an impressive 66 yards.

Kaepernick looked even better the next week against the Chicago Bears. He completed 12 of his first 14 passes. One of those passes was for 57 yards. The throw took both accuracy

Whenever Kaepernick scores a touchdown, he celebrates by kissing his bicep. The celebration has become so popular that people have started calling it "Kaepernicking."

Kaepernick rolls out and throws a pass against the Chicago Bears during the 2012 season.

and strength. It turned out to be the 49ers' longest pass play of the season. San Francisco won the game in a blowout 32–7.

The 49ers won the next week too. That meant San Francisco's coach, Jim Harbaugh, had a difficult decision to make. Smith was fully recovered from his head injury. With Smith in the lineup, the 49ers had won 20 of their last 25 games. He had proven himself to be an excellent quarterback. Then again,

Kaepernick led his San Francisco 49ers to a comeback victory over the Atlanta Falcons in the 2012 conference title game.

Kaepernick had just won two games in a row. He had also made several big plays with his arm and with his feet.

Everybody seemed to have a different opinion on who should be the 49ers' starting quarterback. In the end, Harbaugh decided Kaepernick gave the team the best chance to win the Super Bowl.

Over the next several weeks, Kaepernick had good and bad games. But Harbaugh had made up his mind. Kaepernick was his starter for the rest of the season.

Once the playoffs started, everyone agreed that Harbaugh had made the right decision. Kaepernick proved that in the win over the Green Bay Packers. Then he came up big again on the road against the Atlanta Falcons in the conference title game.

The powerful Falcons flew to a 17–0 lead. Finally, the 49ers started to get things going. Running back Frank Gore scored two touchdowns. The defense stopped the Falcons' offense. And Kaepernick completed 16 of 21 passes. It all added up to an amazing comeback 28–24 victory. The next stop was Super Bowl XLVII.

San Francisco had a new opponent—the Baltimore Ravens. But just like in the Falcons game, the 49ers found themselves behind early. The season looked to be over when Ravens return man Jacoby Jones scored a touchdown to open the second half. Baltimore led 28–6.

Then, all of a sudden, the stadium went dark. A power outage had caused the lights to go out. All the players could do was wait for the backup lights to warm up. They stood and stretched and chatted with each other.

When the lights came back on, it was the 49ers who grabbed the momentum. Kaepernick and his offense began another furious comeback. Wide receiver Michael Crabtree caught a pass from Kaepernick, broke two tackles, and scampered into the end zone. A few minutes later, Gore raced across the goal line from six yards out. The two teams traded field goals. Then Kaepernick scored on a 15-yard run. It was the longest run by a quarterback in Super Bowl history. The score was 31–29. If the 49ers made the two-point conversion, the game would be tied. But Kaepernick's pass fell incomplete.

The Ravens' kicker made a field goal to give his team a five-point lead. San Francisco had one more chance to drive down the field.

A field goal would not be good enough. The 49ers needed a touchdown. Kaepernick brought them all the way to the Ravens' 5-yard line. He had three chances to make the comeback complete. Each pass went to Crabtree. And each pass landed incomplete.

Amazingly, the two head coaches in Super Bowl XLVII were brothers. Jim Harbaugh coached the 49ers. John Harbaugh coached the Ravens. Some started referring to the Super Bowl as the "Harbowl."

Kaepernick makes a pass under pressure against the Baltimore Ravens in Super Bowl XLVII.

After running down the clock and taking a safety, the Ravens were the Super Bowl champions. As disappointed as Kaepernick and his teammates were, their season had been great. Kaepernick had gone from benchwarmer to star. With him taking all the snaps, the future looks bright for the 49ers.

FUN FACTS AND QUOTES

- Colin Kaepernick's hometown, Turlock, California, has a restaurant that named a hot dog after him. "The Kaepernick" includes special sauce, all-meat chili, coleslaw, and jalapenos. Kaepernick himself probably wouldn't order the hot dog, though. He prefers his hot dogs with just a little ketchup.

- Kaepernick is even competitive when he plays board games. His favorite games are Sorry and Catch Phrase.

- When Kaepernick was a child, he was a really picky eater. He did not like to eat much other than Chicken McNuggets and Gummi Bears.

- Kaepernick can throw a football almost 60 miles per hour.

WEB LINKS

To learn more about Colin Kaepernick, visit ABDO Publishing Company online at **www.abdopublishing.com**. Web sites about Kaepernick are featured on our Book Links page. These links are routinely monitored and updated to provide the most current information available.

GLOSSARY

defense
The players on a football team who try to stop the other team's offense from scoring points.

draft
An annual event during which NFL teams select the top college football players.

momentum
A continued strong performance based on recent success.

offense
The players on a football team who control the ball and try to score points.

overtime
In college football, an extra session added to a game if it is tied after regulation in order to determine a winner.

playoffs
A series of games played after the regular season to determine which teams go on to the Super Bowl.

redshirted
When a college athlete sits out a season to gain experience without losing a year of eligibility.

rookie
A first-year player in the NFL.

scholarship
Financial assistance awarded to students to help them pay for college. Top athletes earn scholarships to represent a college through its sports teams.

INDEX

FURTHER RESOURCES

Doeden, Matt. *Tom Brady: Unlikely Champion*. Minneapolis, MN: Twenty-First
    Century Books, 2011.

Lester, Brian. *San Francisco 49ers*. Edina, MN: ABDO Publishing Co., 2011.

Wilner, Barry. *The Super Bowl*. Minneapolis, MN: ABDO Publishing Co., 2013.